noisy

It's very **noisy**!

to~

The dog has a lot of **toys**.

postman

The **postman** is here!

wait

They are **waiting** for the bus.

Where's the popcorn?
Look in your book.
Can you find it?

nickelodeon
SpongeBob SQUAREPANTS

SPONGEBOB'S NEW TOY

SpongeBob is eating breakfast.
'Look, Gary!' he says. 'Eat this **cereal** and
have a **free toy**!'

SpongeBob eats a lot of **cereal**.
Then he goes out.

'What are you doing?' asks Patrick.
'I'm **waiting** for the **postman**!' says
SpongeBob.

'Can I **wait** too?' asks Patrick.

'Yes,' says SpongeBob. 'The **postman** has got my **free toy**!'

SpongeBob and Patrick are very **noisy**! 'Be quiet!' shouts Squidward.

It is August.

'Come and play!' shout SpongeBob's friends.
'No!' says SpongeBob. 'We're **waiting** for
the **postman**!'

It is October.

'Come and play!' shout SpongeBob's friends.
'No!' says Patrick. 'We're **waiting** for the
postman!'

Now it is December.

SpongeBob and Patrick are still **waiting** for the **postman**!

One day, the **postman** comes.
'That's quick!' says Patrick.

'Let's go and see Squidward!' says
SpongeBob.

SpongeBob opens the **free toy**.

'Can I play with it?' asks Patrick.

But the new **toy breaks**.

'MY NEW **TOY**!' shouts SpongeBob.

Squidward **fixes** the **toy**.

'Thank you!' shouts SpongeBob.
'Now be quiet!' says Squidward.

SpongeBob eats a lot of **cereal**.

'I want a **free toy** for Squidward!' he says.

'What are you doing?' shouts Squidward.
'We're **waiting** for the **postman**!' says
SpongeBob.

Not again!

THE END

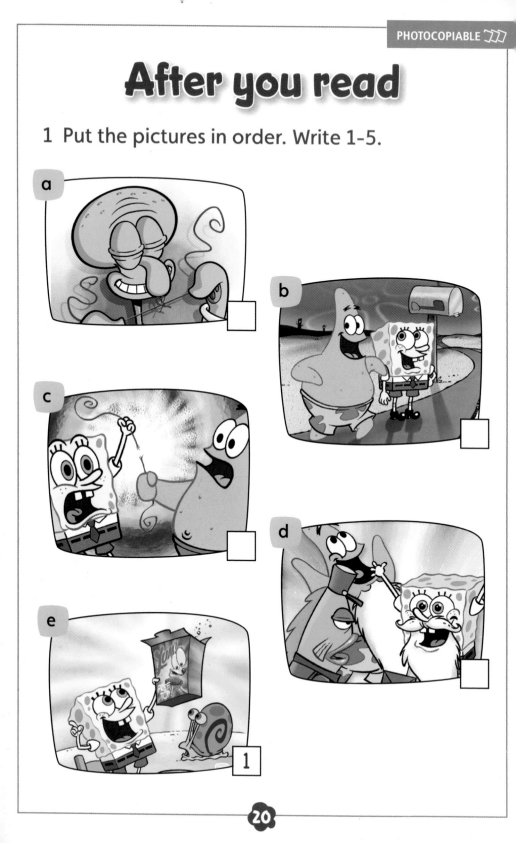

After you read

1 Put the pictures in order. Write 1–5.

a

b

c

d

e [1]

20

2a **Complete the sentences with the words in the box.**

breaks ~~comes~~ fixes opens

a) One day, the postman ...**comes**... .

b) SpongeBob .... the toy.

c) Oh no! The new toy ....

d) Squidward .... SpongeBob's toy.

b **Is SpongeBob sad, happy or very happy? Draw his face on the pictures.**

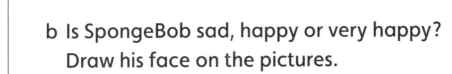

3 Complete the sentences.

This toy is <u>n</u> _ <u>w</u>

Now it's <u>o</u> _ <u>d</u>

It's <u>n</u> _ _ <u>s</u> <u>y</u> !

Now it's _ _ <u>i</u> <u>e</u> <u>t</u>

This postman is <u>s</u> <u>l</u> _ _

Now he's <u>q</u> <u>u</u> _ _ <u>k</u> !

Quiz time!

Answer the questions.

1) What does SpongeBob eat?

☐ dinner   ☐ breakfast

2) What colour are SpongeBob's shoes?

☐ black   ☐ yellow

3) Who has got blue eyes?

☐ Patrick   ☐ SpongeBob

4) Who has got a bag?

☐ the postman   ☐ Squidward

5) What colour is SpongeBob's new toy?

☐ blue   ☐ red

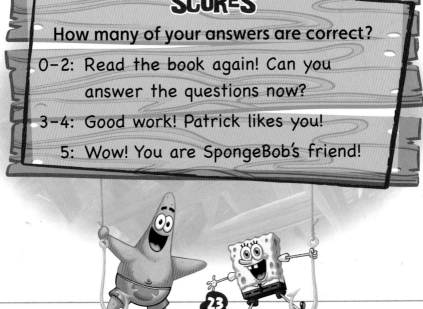

SCORES

How many of your answers are correct?

0–2: Read the book again! Can you answer the questions now?

3–4: Good work! Patrick likes you!

5: Wow! You are SpongeBob's friend!

Chant

1 🎵 **Listen and read.**

I'm waiting

What are you doing?
Come with me, please!

I'm waiting for the postman,
He's got a toy for me.

What are you doing?
Do you want to play?

I'm waiting for the postman,
He's got a toy today.

2 🎵 **Say the chant.**

24